THE PARADOX OF DIVERSITY IN PUBLIC & PRIVATE SECTORS:

Reflections of an African-American Female Educator

By

Dr. Kehinde I. Olowoyeye

2021

The Paradox of Diversity in Public & Private Sectors:

Reflections of an African American Female Educator

Kehinde I. Olowoyeye Ph.D.

First Printing: 2021

ISBN 978-1-6671-6397-0

USA

Ordering Information:

Special discounts are available on quantity purchases by corporations, associations, educators, and others. For details, contact the publisher at the above listed address.

U.S. trade bookstores and wholesalers: Please contact Dr. Kehinde I. Olowoyeye at Kehinde.olowoyeye@cequityec.com

DEDICATION

To my children, Ruthie and Joshua, my North Stars - You inspire me. I will always love you both.

TABLE OF CONTENTS

ACKNOWLEDGMENTS

Thank God Almighty for His grace, mercy, and guidance. Thanks to my amazing and dear friends, Dr. Martha N. Ovando, Natosha Daniels, and Bodunrin Ihonde. They contributed to this book's success through their critical contributions, reviews, and encouragements.

Thanks to my awesome and incredible sister and brother-in-law, Helen and Churchill Kayode, including my wonderful brother, Samuel Fayemiwo, for their support and encouragement.

PREFACE

The recent events and the growing racial-justice movement in the nation have led business sectors and the public workforce, including learning institutions, to rethink diversity in many ways. These organizations and institutions continue to make efforts to improve upon the diversity of their workforce. However, these efforts fail most of the time, even when the best intentions drove the actions because the actions implemented work against the desired outcome. Like other public and private sectors, public school districts' efforts at workforce diversity usually contradict the concept of diversity and inclusion—even if their intentions are otherwise good. An individual or a group can exhibit actions that are contrary to workforce diversity. Some measures that can also contradict workforce diversity are inherent in policies that create systemic racial inequities.

This book carefully explained how individuals, regardless of race, gender, and organizational position, and administrative policies can negatively impact the outcomes of diversity efforts to uphold the dominant culture's ideologies, thereby marginalizing people or educators of color. The book described how public-school leaders' actions and inactions contribute to the diversity efforts' failures. The author used their personal and professional experiences as the lens of critical reflection through which they analyzed the different scenarios described in the book.

This book's intention holds the author's narratives and shares the perspectives of others who have experienced similar circumstances. It describes the author's experiences as a teacher and an administrator in a large Texas school district. This academic exercise is not an indictment nor an expose, but rather an inspiration born out of a need stemming from the much-neglected awareness of racial injustice and thirst for equity in the United States and worldwide. The author has undertaken the painful steps to write this book to draw the attention of leaders in power to the problems at hand—hoping for change to happen.

INTRODUCTION

Diversity's implementations via public efforts in recent history throughout business sectors and the public workforce made headlines and some headway in our society. In those attempts, it should not surprise anyone that failure occurs in these same efforts—even when the best of intentions is seemingly desired. This unfortunate notion is also tantamount to some of our school systems. Public-school districts' efforts at workforce diversity usually contradict the concept of diversity and inclusion—even if their intentions are otherwise good.

The contradictions occur due to intentional and unintentional decision-making and systemic processes that continue to uphold racial inequities. The implicit biases inherent in school districts' hiring practices impede any efforts made to increase the possibilities of hiring educators of color. Likewise, the culture and climate, including the systems and policies in the places mentioned in this effort, are largely emmewed and do not support their vows of retention and progression to administrative or management positions for qualified minority candidates.

Educators of color frequently get "professionally stifled and unsupported" due to the lack of top management access in the education environment. In my experience, campus and district administrators can hold educators of color's emotions in a chokehold with a lack of support. They use these chokeholds as strategies to perpetuate racial injustice. The ideals of a latent or active form of the dominant culture ideologies prevalent in many powerful organizations, including public educational institutions, make thinking about challenging such authority even more disconcerting. The raw power of these suffocating emotions trickles down to affect our students of color in the classrooms. Since the educators (teachers/administrators) that could stand up for what is just and right, are emotionally incapacitated, they may become complacent or compromised instruments weaponized by the system to work against other promising teachers of color (TOC) perceived as too vocal or ardent challengers of backward or status quo policies coupled with racial injustice at this level.

The educators of color coopted unwittingly become compliant out of fear of becoming a target and losing their jobs. Others craving to belong to a white-dominated caucus acquiesce on theirs. They usually pose the greatest threat to diversity. While appearing to be supportive, this group only does so to get close enough to you to know your areas of strengths and weaknesses to undermine and marginalize you. Also, they exhibit some elements of the famed crab mentality, kicking you back down to stop you from speaking out for equitable conditions for educators and students of color.

This book's intention holds my narratives and shares the perspectives of others who have experienced similar circumstances. It describes my experiences as a teacher and an administrator in a large Texas school district. This academic exercise is not an indictment nor an expose, but rather an inspiration born out of a need stemming from the much-neglected awareness of racial injustice and thirst for equity in the United States and worldwide. I have undertaken the painful steps to write this book to draw the attention of those in power to the problems at hand—hoping for change to happen.

Realizing my experiences' totality, I wish to encourage others who may be undergoing similar involvements illustrated here to let them know they are not alone. This book describes the impediments I encountered and how these same obstacles prevented me from exercising my diverse skills to benefit the organization moving forward. It also includes the implicit and explicit biases that influenced how campus and district administrators conceived and implemented policies.

I also narrated the backlashes and consequences I experienced for standing and speaking for what is right and just for educators of color and our students. As I continue to pass through these challenges, I have learned that educators of color in power either become complacent or volunteer to uphold racial injustice to keep their positions. They do this at the expense of our Black and Latinx students. In this book, I described the roles I played and continue to play as a Black immigrant educator, advocating for what is just and right for all students, especially for students of color.

As an immigrant African American educator, I went into education to influence all students' lives and ensure all students get equitable opportunities to be successful. All immigrant Africans encounter institutional racial inequities that have been in existence for centuries, with an added layer of being an immigrant. As we make our stance known and speak against systemic racism in all sectors, we are bound to experience some backlashes and consequences to varying degrees.

Before I share my story, I'm using this platform to apologize openly from my heart's depth to all my African American sisters and brothers for all Africans' roles in slavery. My words may not be enough to take away the pains. However, I'm hoping you all would allow me to use this platform to express that I'm standing with you and have been since I immigrated to the United States.

To all my African immigrant sisters and brothers, I call on you to reflect on how we show our appreciation to all our African American sisters and brothers. We must continue to respect and appreciate the fight fought before we got here. At the same time, stand together to ensure we speak against all acts of racism and inequities in our communities and workplaces.

I will share some pertinent background information about myself before explaining what I went through and how campus and district administrators affected me emotionally & professionally.

Growing up in Nigeria, I completed my PreK-12 schooling, then my undergraduate and postgraduate education work focusing on Botany. I worked as an assistant lecturer at the University of Lagos (UNILAG), Nigeria, from 1997-1999 before leaving the country for Dublin, Ireland. Enrolling in the doctorate program in Botany at the University College Dublin (UCD), I researched the "Effects of Low Temperature on Maize." I relocated to the United States with my family in 2004 through the visa lottery program. My desire to know more about the educational system and teach in the United States led me to enroll in a second master's program.

In the fall of 2004, I chose education with a concentration in Biology as my focus at Lincoln University, Philadelphia, PA. My family moved with me to Baltimore, MD, in the fall of 2005. A teaching position opened up with Baltimore City Public School (BCPSS) through the alternative teacher certification program offered by BCPSS in partnership with Johns Hopkins University. I attended classes for the teacher certification concurrently with the master's program in Philadelphia with my hiring.

My first year teaching in the inner-city of Baltimore was very challenging. Although I had a clinical professor that observed me monthly and gave feedback, I wouldn't have gained more insight into the community if it wasn't for my mentor teacher. She took me on a ride around the school's neighborhood to help me understand our students. The majority of the houses around the school were group homes. She explained that I needed to learn how to make my students trust me by empathizing with them. Most of the students did not believe in adults and educators because of their past experiences. Realizing this hard truth, I changed my approach and teaching philosophy to better meet my students' needs. The act of driving around the neighborhood and the conversation with Ms. M resulted in a mind-shift that enabled me to connect practice with theory. I became restless throughout that day after exploring the community with her. I thought about my students, our interactions, and what I could do to make it better. After this, I became intentional with the way I related to my students and my expectations.

The following Monday, I apologized for my over-zealousness to all my students in each class period. In the classroom, my emphasis centered on the importance of education without fully understanding their needs and why it was vital for them to understand me. I told them about myself knowing they have an internal curiosity (perhaps unspoken) to understand my passion for education and what drives me. Sharing my experiences as a teenager was very emotional. However, I needed to let my students know that I empathize with them.

Starting with the loss of my father on the last day of December, two weeks after turning sixteen in high school, revealed a lot. His death shattered my hopes, along with my love for education. My father was fortunate and had the opportunity to attend a two-year college and gained employment as an accountant in different government organizations. On the other hand, my mother did not have the privilege to go beyond elementary school. The patriarchal argument then was that educating girls was a waste of money and resources since they would end up in a man's home and kitchen. Despite my mom's background, she treasured education and wanted me and my siblings to attain a measure of education. My parents had nine children that included four sets of twins. Two of us are females, my older sister and me. Within our family, the world turned upside down as soon as our dad left this earth. Facing a new unwelcomed reality, Mom sold clothes, the few jewelry pieces she had to feed us, to pay for my older brothers and sister to complete their education. They, in turn, struggled to get jobs to support the rest of us.

Losing my father caused me immense frustration and depression. My solid rock, my foundation—the one person that encouraged me to study—was gone. This new uncertainty of what the future held for me led to rebellion. Skipping high school classes and hiding under a secluded tree became my refuge. Much to my student's surprise, my ditching class ended thanks to my math teacher's efforts, Mr. Suleiman. He took it upon himself with other teachers' help to ensure I got my homework done during lunch or physical education. This educational system provided me with the extra support I needed until my confidence to succeed was reborn.

However, things at home didn't get any better financially. The hardship was so much to bear that we barely had two meals a day. On a particularly difficult day, out of near starvation and hopelessness, my sister and I made a pact that we would pursue higher education and have fewer kids. Knowing the power of education and how it is key in opening doors of opportunity—we set forth on achieving our plan. Once you have attained those degrees and all that comes with them—no one can strip you of the knowledge you acquire—only if you decide to share it. As women, we wanted to be self-reliant and not experience our mom's hopelessness after our father passed away.

Sharing this story with my students let them know, I too had a vulnerable side. I used the opportunity to tell them that I empathized with them because experiencing hardships was something we had in common. Dissuading them from the damage teachers in their past had inflicted intentionally or intentionally was my next bridge to cross. I introduced some aspects to look for in a genuine teacher. I wanted them to know sincere educators pull students up when they are down by providing the most appropriate and equitable support to ensure their success. My students made the connection to the understanding that I identified with them and their struggles while holding them accountable for every assignment. At this point, we had a breakthrough in understanding. They finally trusted me in sharing their experiences. We discussed our classroom norms regarding what they wanted from me and what I expected from them. Our relationships and rapport improved and blossomed and created a respectful and safe learning environment.

An example of the things we agreed upon was what my students should do when upset and unable to participate, especially when they are frustrated about anything. The expectation was that they should write their emotions on a sticky note to let me know. In reaction to what they wrote, I gave them space to cool off. However, I expected that they would come during lunch or after school to complete the work they missed in class. I provided peanut butter crackers and water to the students who came to class without breakfast and gave them time to eat while getting their work done. Each year, I looked for different ways to build the right relationships and trust with my students while holding them accountable to ensure their success. My experiences as a Black immigrant educator in Baltimore were vastly different from my experiences in Texas. With my family moving to Texas in 2008, I came down south for a few job fairs that most school districts in Texas offered before permanently relocating in July.

Attending these job fairs gave me an excellent personal glimpse into how implicit and explicit biases inherent in hiring practices continue to close the doors on educators of color. Every school principal I met and shared my resume with refused to engage with me. Those that talked to me were not friendly. They gave me the cold shoulder. After attending a district's job fair and not even getting an audience one time, I sat outside the event fair, crying out of frustration after almost everyone had left. An African American woman saw me crying and walked over. She asked me what I was doing, sitting there alone, and weeping. I explained to her that I'd attended several job fairs, and this was my last hope, as my family had just relocated to Texas.

To my surprise, she requested my resume. As soon as she saw my name, she exclaimed, "This is the name nobody wanted to call or pronounce (Kehinde Olowoyeye)!"

She stated that although my credentials indicated I was qualified for the job, my name deterred school principals from inviting me for an interview. Having an idea why the school principals ignored me or acted the way they did during the job fair made me sad. I cried so much that my heart hurt. The woman took my resume and told me to expect a call later that day. She made time to talk and get to know me taking a bold step to pull me up from where others kept me down. That same day, an assistant principal (AP) called me to schedule me for an interview the next day. They offered me the position of a high school science intervention teacher.

My first few weeks working on this high school campus, even before the students started that fall semester in 2008, unlocked the door to my racial consciousness. The first science department meeting was a shock to me. I noticed I was the only Black teacher amongst over thirty educators. They all avoided sitting next to me when they walked into the meeting. The AP introduced the new hires, a master teacher, and me. The master teacher was a White woman that came from another Texas school district. The department accepted and welcomed her warmly. As soon as the AP introduced me as the intervention teacher, they all looked at each other and laughed scornfully. As I stood in their midst and talked about myself, I felt most unwelcome. A few of the teachers claimed that their students would not understand me, and they would rather not have me come to their classroom to help the students. A detailed description of the events between the teachers and me is in the next chapter.

The purpose of writing this book is to inform practicing school district administrators, including universities and colleges preparing future educators, of the impact of policies and systemic racial inequities that happen in real-time to teachers and administrators of color. I hope the scenarios narrated in the following chapters would elicit discussions amongst student bodies and professors who teach future educators, principals, and superintendent preparation programs. At the end of each chapter, I posed a few thought-provoking questions to spark fervent classroom conversation. Finally, my desire in this wholehearted effort is to educate district and campus administrators, human resources, counselors, and district legal departments on how to implement equitable policies.

The next four chapters highlight the different challenges I encountered as a Black immigrant intervention teacher and then as an administrator in the same department. I also described how I continue to navigate the various, emotionally stifling obstacles present in each position.

HOW TOKENISM CREATES ISOLATION AND NON-INCLUSIVENESS

School district leaders continue to make some efforts to promote workforce diversity by showing they are improving on recruiting teachers and administrators of color. However, the hiring practices and the autonomy given to campus leaders and department leads in the district offices impede the diversity efforts because of the implicit and explicit biases inherent in the practices. The few educators of color hired are sparingly located on various campuses and offices within the district, creating a sense of aloneness or isolation. Although district and campus leaders intend to promote workforce diversity, the hiring structure ultimately produces a false sense of racial equality and tokenism across the district. My 'token' experience and racial consciousness as a Black immigrant educator in a Texas school will clarify this discourse.

As I reflected on my three years of service in Baltimore, I realized that the educators I worked with had their biases just like everybody else. However, they did not overtly question my race and nationality, nor deprived me of the opportunity to contribute to students' education in a meaningful way. In a worrisome contrast, my existence and contributions to the educational system as a Black immigrant continues to be questioned in this Texas district. I was the only African American teacher in the science department in 2008. I believe we had about five Black teachers and one Black assistant principal in the whole school, consisting of over ninety teachers and seven administrators.

Before I describe my first-year experience in detail, it is essential to provide contextual, demographic data. When I started teaching in 2008, Black teachers' representation in the entire district was only 3%, approximately 83 Black teachers compared to 277 and 2,386 Hispanic and White teachers. The number of Black teachers in the whole district was below 100 until 2015, 3.7% with 120 Black teachers. It slowly increased to 4% in 2016. The district maintained this rate until 2018. The data shows that the district's hiring practices are not in sync with the ideology of hiring teachers or staff representing their student demography. The population of Black students was between 9 and 11%. This data also explains why we had about five Black teachers and one Black administrator on that campus in 2008. I felt isolated in my department, and the teachers did not hide that they didn't accept me.

As briefly explained in chapter one, the White teachers sabotaged my efforts to perform the original position as an intervention teacher that the school hired me to do in 2008. Whenever I walked into their classrooms, they usually asked me to step into the hallway to talk to me. They expressed multiple times that they did not want me to help their students and that the students would have difficulty understanding me. When I voiced my concerns to the department chair, a White teacher, she told me she would talk to the AP and do something about my assignment. The AP reassigned me to the credit recovery class to assist the three teachers and two teacher assistants that taught the online courses. I taught science subjects to students enrolled in credit recovery classes.

In January of 2009, the science department chair informed me that both she and the AP have decided to give me a chance to teach a biology trailer course. The students that failed the first semester of biology took the trailer course to relearn the content taught in the first semester and concurrently took the second-semester biology. They also enrolled students that failed the previous year's biology Texas Assessment of Knowledge and Skills (TAKS) exam in the trailer class. A few weeks after the class started, my students told me that the department chair and the AP called a few of them to the office to check their notes and asked if they understood my accent and learned. The students reported that they told them they understood my accent and were grasping the concepts better. As the teaching progressed, I retaught the first-semester content. I weaved in the second semester to prepare them for the TAKS exam. Almost all my students passed the TAKS exam, including those that took it the second time. The TAKS data convinced the department chair and the AP that I was capable of teaching successfully.

At the end of the 2008 - 2009 school year, the department chair called me into her classroom to talk about my first year. She started by apologizing for the way the whole department treated me. A female teacher started the hateful narrative regarding their fears that the students would not understand my accent. Others joined in without giving me a chance. She further stated that she felt terrible and guilty as a Christian that she contributed to the mistreatment. I told her that I accepted her apology and appreciated that she reflected and conversed with me, knowing it was difficult. She stated that she pleaded on my behalf with the AP to teach biology (four sections per A & B-days) the next school year. Again, at the end of the 2009 - 2010 and 2010 - 2011 school years, the number of my students that passed the biology TAKS exam outweighed other teachers that taught biology.

An unusual event took place in the 2011 - 2012 school year. The Black female assistant principal became the first Black principal of the school. It was an iconic event since the school's establishment, which was a century old at the time. That same year, she appointed me the biology professional learning community (PLC) lead due to my record of higher student achievement rates. Sure enough, our school's biology scores on the STAAR exam were impressive, second in the district by a margin, less than 1% compared to the school that had always led the district.

In 2010, I enrolled for a third master's degree in Educational Administration at The University of Texas at Austin (UT) to better understand the system. I also did this to navigate the different obstacles and deal with the overt rejection and racial discrimination that I continued to encounter daily. Needing to find an outlet to ease the pain I felt, this process gave me a better understanding of the system and the people that worked with me. The UT Principalship Program inspired me and provided context regarding what social justice leaders do. In 2011- 2012, I conducted Participatory Action Research (PAR). It was one of the principalship program graduation requirements. I identified a problem of practice: the lack of access given to students of color to enroll in Advanced Placement (AP) courses. Over the four years of teaching in the school, I noticed that most of our students of color were not in both Pre-AP and AP classes. I was troubled and curious to know why this was so.

When the opportunity to investigate a problem of practice on my campus arose through the principalship program, I talked to the new Black female principal for consent. She accepted, and I wrote the proposal to get district approval to conduct the study. I invited four other teachers to represent the three racial groups (Black, Hispanic, and White). They also taught on-level, Pre-AP, and AP classes. We created survey questions for teachers, counselors, students, and parents to know why we had a low enrollment of students of color each year. The findings gathered from the survey responses indicated that the school policies, such as teachers that acted as "gatekeepers," including the messages and marketing strategies, discouraged students and parents from enrolling in the classes. The principal and the rest of the administrative team implemented the suggestion we (PAR team) provided. The rates of enrollment of students of color increased.

The study's success and the biology PLC's achievement on the STAAR exam allowed me to apply for the same school's assistant principal position in 2012. The Black female principal told me that my ability to lead the team and my records of accomplishment convinced her I could perform an administrator's role. A couple of

21

the administrators pushed back at the idea. I was so excited and grateful for the opportunity! Imagine a Black immigrant (Nigerian) not accepted by her department when she started in 2008—becoming the supervising administrator to those same teachers that rejected her—in 2012. Obadiah himself would be proud!

My first year as an AP was very challenging and, at the same time, a great learning experience. At the end of the 2012 - 2013 school year, some of the teachers I supervised in the science department transferred to other schools within the district because they could not continue taking directives or accepting management from a supervisor of color. The vacant positions allowed me to hire new teachers whose philosophy aligned with the department and campus using an equity lens, with the other teachers' help in the department.

Working late into most nights during the week to meet deadlines came at the cost of my family's expense. It was a burden to bear. Nevertheless, I did this because I needed to perform beyond expectations and prove to the admin team and the teachers that I could effectively perform my roles regardless of race and nationality. A couple of assistant principals (AP's) told me I would soon burn out if I continued working late and that my family would suffer. At the time, I knew they said those things because they saw me as a threat even though there was an element of truth in what they said. I focused on getting my work done before them and strived to be better at it.

Tokenism within an organization with a culture and climate that is not inclusive creates tension and the need for the tokenized individual to perform better in response to the predominant group's implicit and explicit biases. The environment eventually causes emotional and mental stress on the educator of color, with the option to conform to the dominant culture or continue to operate in a constant state of emotional stress. To survive these unwelcome environments and progress in leadership roles, some educators of color conform and represent the system's weapons to subdue other educators of color. In the next chapter, I narrated my experiences with the Black female principal. I also shared my interpretation and perceptions of the roles she played as a weapon against another Black educator to uphold the dominant culture's ideals. The power dynamics between her and her subordinates, including me, created inequities and fear.

CHAPTER 2 DISCUSSION QUESTIONS

- What do you think the science department chair and the assistant principal could have done differently to ensure that other department members accepted the intervention teacher?

- What do you think the science department chair and the assistant principal could have done differently to ensure the intervention teacher performed her duties without barriers?

- Imagine you were the new teacher, a Black immigrant with a Nigerian accent and name. What would you do to be accepted by the members of the department to get your work done?

- How would you feel if nothing you did could change the other teachers' perspectives, and they bluntly expressed they do not welcome you in their classes?

HOW THE ACTIONS OF LEADERS OF COLOR UPHOLD THE IDEOLOGIES OF THE DOMINANT CULTURE

School districts, like other organizations, also create tokenized leadership positions for educators of color. Most of these leaders of color initially strive to disrupt the systemic racial inequities but eventually get tired of being isolated. They can become unwittingly coopted and ultimately become compliant out of fear of becoming a target that could result in losing their jobs. Other leaders of color can be ruthless, driven by the need to be in power, and their actions could continue to support the dominant culture's ideologies. In chapter two, the Black female principal I mentioned fits into the second group of educators of color that are ruthless and are weapons used to uphold whiteness. These leaders perpetuate racial inequities against subordinates of color. The decisions and actions of this second group of leaders of color can be destructive to the lives of their victims, especially when they have a personal bias, prejudice, or vendetta towards the individual. The extent to which they would go to destroy the individual is dependent on the person leading the school system's human resources and the relationship they have with them. Besides, these leaders use the district's policies created from whiteness's lens as excuses to promote inequitable behaviors and decision-making.

The Black female principal hired her assistant principals, including me, with the intent to control, viewing her subordinates' weaknesses from a deficit mindset, regardless of their strengths. She shared with us that she intentionally hired us with characteristics perceived as deficits. The principal expressed that our shortcomings prevented other principals from hiring us. Her actions and words indicated she demanded we likened and saw her as our "savior" for hiring us, and we should be indebted to her forever. Her actions and words embodied "The White Saviorism Syndrome," although she is Black. My Nigerian accent was what she focused on as a shortcoming based on the challenges I encountered with the teachers when I started as an educator. She also expressed her perceptions of the other assistant principals. She commented on their weight, inability to give a presentation in front of a crowd due to anxiety, and one AP that never accomplished any tasks on time. However, the AP was very good at scheduling, a skill set needed by the team. This principal rarely focused on our strengths.

As assistant principals, we all felt stuck, indebted to her, and fearful of what she could do to destroy our careers. We knew she was capable of preventing us from moving on to become campus principals. Undoubtedly, she was a strong instructional leader and also a ruthless individual that stated she loved to compete to win—whatever it takes. She also boastfully expressed that none of us can progress, except she approved it. Most days, she lashed out at us. By her command—none of us could leave or apply for principal positions without her consent. The teachers and other staff members constantly remained terrified of her. One of the White female APs told me that she had a conversation with the principal a day after she castigated us on a specific occasion. The White AP told the principal that she treated us like battered wives because the principal took us out for dinner after each abuse episode.

Notwithstanding, my trust and loyalty to her were unwavering despite the unfair treatments. I did not want to disappoint her in any way and would always stand up for her and make excuses when others complained to let them know she meant well. However, I began to experience the direct doses of her unkindness and controlling behavior when I started my doctorate program in the fall of 2014 at The University of Texas at Austin.

My experiences with the principal gave me a deeper understanding of how people of color can work against each other out of spite. The Black female principal represented educators of color that make themselves available as instruments to stifle other educators of color. The system uses them to repress other people of color to uphold the dominant culture's ideologies inherent in the system. Remember, I stated earlier that the principal loved to compete to win. She was overbearing and very controlling; and wanted to know what was going on in everybody's lives, classrooms, and offices. It felt like she ruled with a steely fist and used her sledgehammer to knock anyone out of her path. It was either her way or the highway.

The doctorate program issue started in December 2013 during one of our long-drawn admin meetings led by our principal. She shared a letter sent to all district principals regarding one of the major universities' doctorate programs. The principal asked if we would like to enroll. The district was encouraging educators to be life-long learners. Everyone on the team expressed they would pass on the opportunity for various personal reasons. However, I told the team I was interested in applying. The team was not surprised I was interested; they knew how much education meant to me. I had shared why I became an educator one day when we all shared our whys of education in a group setting. They knew my background. In one of our meetings, I shared my mother's upbringing and lack of education and my family's struggles growing up after my dad's death. My cohorts knew how much I invested in educating myself and my children. I held the principal as an ally, even with her overbearing ways. She was very much aware of all the values I held dear. This woman also knew the struggles I was going through at home with a patriarchal husband that was not fully supportive of my educational pursuit.

After the meeting, I stayed back to talk to my principal about my interest in applying for the doctoral program. There was still a remaining issue about the need to speak with my husband (now ex), given his attitude. The principal said I should let her know my decisions and if she needed to give a reference. Officially, I applied for The University of Texas at Austin (UT) and another major university's doctoral programs in Texas. The institutions graciously offered me admissions. Accepting The University of Texas at Austin's doctoral program's offer was practical. I knew commuting the distance to the second university would be challenging. The probable strikes against me from my principal would be the time I took from work and her approval of my departure early from campus. My hunches were right. I discussed the possibilities with my principal since both colleges offered most of the courses in the morning or afternoon, plus considering travel time. Of course, she was not in support of me leaving early to attend the second university. So, in May 2014, I emailed the university to decline the offer. The content of my email was:

Due to work commitments and conflicts, I would like to request a withdrawal from the ED-School Improvement Doctoral Program. I sincerely apologize for any inconvenience caused by this decision. Thank you. Kehinde Olowoyeye.

After we got back to work in July 2014 from the summer break, I informed the principal I registered for my first fall 2014 classes. I shared my class schedule, the times, and the days of the week with my principal to let her know when I would be leaving campus. Afterward, she called me to her office for a meeting to let me know she will not allow me to go to my classes. She also said that the district did not want the staff to take courses that interfered with work time. I pleaded with her and inquired about other district staff in doctoral programs, both in the admin office and other campuses, and why their bosses granted them the opportunity. I also stated that if the district was pushing for us to be lifelong learners, why would they not give us the time to enroll and attend classes? When she realized my determination to continue my academic pursuit, she gave me some demanding parameters to discourage me. They were:

1. I must never register for classes without her consent. Before I registered for classes, I had to show her the required and electives courses, including the schedules with class times and dates. She also demanded the records of all the courses I already took or course requirements previously fulfilled as I progressed.

2. She will choose the courses I register for—the dates and time I'm allowed to leave had to coincide with the two half-days time off per week.

3. I will put in for sick or personal leave days for the two half-days a week regardless of the time I left campus. My principal knew that I would lose my full paycheck once I've depleted the ten days of sick and local leave days allowed each year.

4. So, the fourth parameter was the kicker. The principal mandated that I work on Saturdays to make up for the two half-days I already paid for using my sick or personal allotments. My salary took a hit as the end of the school year approached, after using my sick and personal days.

I had no choice but to agree to all these terms to achieve my dreams. Hurt and sickened by all the principal's efforts—one who was supposed to be a friend—to stop me from enrolling in the doctoral program—kept me motivated. The principal gave excuses that she had to follow these made-up rules to let the other APs know she didn't extend extra privileges to me. She also clamored about needing to get human resources (HR) involved to confirm if I could start my classes. She blind copied me on the email she sent to the Acting HR Executive Director at the time. The content of the email went something like this:

(Name of the acting HR Executive Director), one of my administrators is taking doctoral classes at UT. Her schedule is Monday 4–7 pm and Thursday 1–7 pm. I just wanted to know if there are any limitations and how the district would like us to

handle this situation. She has agreed to work Saturdays from 9-12. Is this allowable? I appreciate all your guidance. Thanks as always!

During our admin meeting that day, the principal shared with the rest of the admin team that she met with me. That the condition she gave me was, I had to take sick or personal half-days to attend graduate classes. A couple of the APs mentioned that others in the district they knew did not use their sick or personal days if they left towards the end of the day. They also did not take sick or personal days if they worked extra hours to make up. One of the administrators asked the principal—what about those working in the district administrative offices that attend graduate classes that do not take sick or personal days? The APs more or less expressed their displeasure at the parameters the principal put forward. They offered to help me out when there were any student or parent emergencies while I was off-campus.

I waited patiently for days to know what the verdict was on the email the principal sent to the HR Acting Executive Director. I was under so much stress and was anxious, not knowing if they would grant me the opportunity. A week later, the principal told me HR consented to the request. I started my classes in August of 2014, took sick and personal half-days, worked on Saturdays as agreed. Based on our agreement, I left campus at about 3:45 pm, twenty-five minutes before the school day ended for the classes I attended on Mondays from 4:00 -7:00 pm. On Thursdays, I left campus at noon for the 1:00 pm classes.

I'm sure most of you reading this may be thinking about this question. Why would I agree to work on Saturdays to make up the hours already deducted when I could spend the time with my family and do graduate homework? Yes, that is true! It was a necessary sacrifice for me.

On Saturdays, I left home at 8:30 am to complete work assigned to me by the principal and those on my to-do list for the week. For example, I completed all the paperwork for each 504-accommodation meetings I conducted during the week. I prepared documents for the following week's 504 meetings. I called parents on different issues and worked on data that I needed to share with my teachers. Some days, I left at noon or later, depending on the work I needed to finish. Once I got home, I took my children for their Kumon math and reading lessons. The center opened at 11:00 am, but we usually arrived at about 12:30 or 1:00 pm. I got some house chores or my graduate school homework done in three to four hours before picking my children up at 4:30 pm.

We prepared dinner as soon as we got home, talked, and had some family time before bedtime. I resumed my work schedule to complete graduate homework once everybody was safely in bed. I also became the backup alarm for my children, woke them up to get homework done. It was a difficult time, but I stayed the course. Now I can say that the principal's intention to discourage me fueled my desire to accomplish my goals. It helped my children learn and experience how tenacity and perseverance help with achievement.

Based on the principal's terms of the agreement, I consulted with her before I registered for the spring semester for approval. She approved me to register for a morning statistics class (9:00 am - 12:00 pm), only offered at that time, and another course offered on a different day in the afternoon. On the days I had the morning classes, I left from home and resumed work at 1:00 pm. I used my sick or personal days and made up the three hours I was off-campus on Saturdays. On completing the fall semester in December of 2014, a personal tragedy struck. I lost my mom on December 28th, which hit me hard. Going back to work in January, I carried a lot of pain and grief, but I could not take time off to mourn properly. I needed to save my sick and personal days for the two-week travel to Nigeria to attend my mom's funeral at the end of January 2015. I also needed the days to go to my graduate classes based on the initial agreement I had with the principal. I couldn't take time off to grieve. After much

31

thought and planning, I knew that the only way to finish my graduate classes was to enroll in the two summer sessions each year. The decision saved me from taking more years and half-days.

I enrolled for the initial summer offering of classes in May of 2015. The principal reprimanded me for not consulting with her during one of our admin meetings after students and teachers left for the summer break. Assistant principals' contracts usually extended a couple of weeks after the students' and teachers' left for the summer holiday, and I thought I could register for my summer classes. The principal was not happy with me. I apologized and pleaded for permission to attend my classes the first two weeks of the initial summer session. She reluctantly agreed. I was so relieved after those two weeks ended. Freedom in hand, I was glad about having the liberty to register for the second summer session without her controlling and probing questions. As the fall semester of 2015 rolled around, my anxiety kicked in, knowing I had to go through the same grueling conditions imposed on me by my so-called friend and boss. Nevertheless, I summoned up the courage and with a strong sense of self-motivation and faith that if I could make the first year with God's help—I could do it again in year two!

I scheduled the time to meet with the principal to discuss my fall 2015 registration. She complimented me for completing my first year. However, she made a statement that gave me a reason to pause and think.

She said, "Anyone can complete the coursework as fast as you are trying to. The only thing that holds such people back from achieving in the doctoral program is dissertation writing. So, don't get all excited that you are moving fast through the classes."

I noted her words, knowing that the bible says that from the abundance of the heart, the mouth speaketh Matthew 12:34 (KJV). I understood that I would go through a more difficult and challenging time with her attempts to break me—I persevered. At the same time, I struggled to figure out why she acted the way she did; and gave myself every excuse in the world not to hold any of these actions against her. I also felt indebted to her for the opportunity she gave me to become an assistant principal. Therefore, I remained loyal and continued to stand up for her, got my job done diligently, and worked extra hours.

When it was time to register for the spring semester in March 2015, I consulted with the principal again. She decided on the classes I took and on the days she wanted me to request half-days. As the STAAR testing rolled around in April 2015, an incident happened that changed our working relationship. The principal called me on a Saturday after I left work as I drove my children to Kumon. The principal stated that one of my teachers, Ms. J, called the assistant principal that coordinated the STAAR testing to inform them that she was sick that weekend. She would not be in school to administer the test on Monday and requested a substitute teacher. My principal wanted me to write the teacher up. To clarify what she expected me to write in the memo and make sense of what she asked me to do, I asked her what the teacher's offense was. I was confused; I couldn't understand how calling in sick during state testing was against the campus or district policy. We cannot control when we fall ill. The principal got so mad at me on the phone that she said, if I can't write the memo, she will ask so-and-so (the AP coordinating testing) to write the teacher up. She then hung up on me before I could explain myself. I knew I was definitely in trouble.

When I got to work the following week, I felt the hostility in the principal's interactions with me. Unfortunately for me, it was the same period I needed to register for the summer one classes. I required her consent since the AP contract extended two weeks beyond students' and teachers' start of the summer break. When I got into the principal's office, she told me she was busy and could not talk to me about my registration. I explained to her that the deadline was in a few days. She said, okay, we can meet later. She evaded me, and I was unable to talk to her that day.

33

The next day, as I approached her in the hallway and asked if I could meet with her regarding my summer one registration, she yelled at me in front of teachers and students.

Lashing out, she said, "I cannot do things for you if you cannot do things for me."

I was stunned and embarrassed that the principal could yell at me publicly.

When the principal noticed my astonishment and that students and teachers in the hallway looked at us in horror, she invited me into her office. When we got there, she stated that she called me to write a teacher up, and I didn't. Why did I think she would allow me to continue with my graduate classes? I didn't know how to respond to her question and told her that I was not clear what the teacher had done wrong and why they wanted me to write her up. My statement made her mad all over again. She pointed out that each day I took half-days or left twenty-five minutes early, she and the other APs picked up after me. She stated that she would not be able to allow me to attend graduate school again. I responded that I got all my work done. I took care of all discipline issues. The admin team occasionally helped with emergencies that occurred while I was off-campus, the same way I supported others when they were off-campus. I conducted all of my students' 504 meetings. I promptly completed their accommodation paperwork, even though I had the highest number of students in the alpha assigned to me compared to the other APs.

My principal responded that she knew I completed everything assigned to me promptly and came on Saturdays. However, she will still not grant me the opportunity to attend graduate classes in the fall of 2016. After I pleaded for some minutes, she gave me two options:

1. I should resign so I could finish my doctorate program, or
2. Stop my doctorate program and keep my job.

I asked them why she would want me to resign when other people, including her, attended and still attend graduate classes.

She said, "I gave you this position, and by God, I can take it from you!"

I was stunned when I heard this statement. I remembered that she told me that she offered me the job based on my performance and potential. I knew she told me the truth when I started as an AP. She was highly ambitious and wouldn't bring on anyone that would not deliver or move numbers in her favor. I reminded her that I gave more than 200% of my time before starting the doctoral program. Then I clarified if she suggested I resign because I could not put in the 200% although I gave 150%. The principal said yes, I had the option to resign or drop out of the doctoral program. Her condition made no sense! She asked me to leave her office, go online to the HR's website to complete my resignation.

Crestfallen, I left her office with a heavy heart, torn and confused. I then called a confidant in the district office to tell him about my plight. He asked if I wanted to file a grievance against the principal, and I said no. He probed further about why I refused to file the complaint. I explained to him that the principal, at the time, was my mentor and closest friend. Also, I was indebted to her for the opportunity to be an assistant principal in a district I would not have had the chance as a Black immigrant female educator. He responded that he understood and advised me to contact human resources to request a one-year leave-of-absence rather than resign from my position.

I checked the district policy to understand the requirement and called my husband (now my ex) to get his support for a year. He agreed to the plan. I then called the new HR Executive Director (HR ED) to schedule a meeting with them later that day. My meeting with the HR ED went well. They wanted to know why I requested the one-year leave-of-absence and if anything happened between the principal and me. I explained that nothing happened and that we were friends, and I respected them. When the HR official probed further to fish for information, I responded that we had the same vision for the campus when I started as an AP. However, my desire to complete my doctorate was no longer in alignment with the principal's view. The only way to accomplish my dreams was to request a one-year leave-of-absence to complete all course work in the 2016-2017 school year. The HR official told me I qualified for the professional development leave-of-absence without pay or benefits. Thankfully, they agreed to take it to the Superintendent and the Board for approval. I left the district office for the campus, hopeful that the Superintendent and the Board would grant me the request.

Upon getting to my office, the administrative assistant told me the principal came looking for me and called about 30 minutes before my arrival. I went to her office, and she asked if I had gone to the district to request a leave-of-absence without her consent. I apologized that I did not know I had to get her permission before going to HR. I told her that I thought it would be a better alternative to the resignation option. She then dismissed me from her office, obviously mad at me. She called a team meeting that day. We had many things we needed to work on before leaving for the summer break in preparation for the beginning of the next school year. As the meeting progressed at about 5:00 pm, the principal excused herself, and we all thought she went to get dinner. She came back after about an hour and told us she went to her car to make an urgent call. I suspected the call was about me to the HR Executive Director, knowing they were friends. However, when I got home that night, I was in for an unwelcome surprise!

The principal and a so-called friend called my husband and talked him into forcing me to resign. In chapter one and earlier in this chapter, I mentioned people of color sometimes volunteer as instruments and weapons to uphold the dominant culture's ideologies. This principal was a classic example and remained one in their current position (more details in the next chapter). Her personal bias made her vindictive to the point that she cared less about what was just and right. She saw me as a competitor she needed to remove from the scene. She was ready to go to any length to achieve her aim. She knew me so well, posed as a close friend, and then stabbed. Metaphorically, she did not stab me in the back, with the opportunity to turn and see who stabbed me—but she put the jagged blade between my neck and shoulder, making it impossible to turn my head.

As soon as I got home, my husband told me the principal, who he referred to as my friend, called him to talk about the leave-of-absence I discussed with him earlier that day. He stated the principal explained the consequences of the leave-of-absence to him better and advised him. The principal informed him that my decision would affect our family's finances, and the burden would be on him. She told him the two options she gave me and wanted him to discourage me from getting the leave-of-absence. She wanted him to force me to either resign or continue working and drop out of graduate school. My husband then asked me which of the two options was I going to take, resign, or stop the doctoral program and continue working? I told him I would not decide until HR gets back to me. I also reminded him that I had single-handedly supported the family before and never complained. I expected him to stand by me. The whole situation added to the strain in my family and exacerbated the ongoing issues at home.

All night, I thought about my next plan of action and what I could do to make the principal grant me the opportunity to work and attend graduate classes. As much as I did not want to upset our friendship, I felt caged and controlled; and realized that she was not my friend. I knew the principal was playing a mind-game on me, my husband, and even the HR Executive Director. I understood the principal's way of dealing with people; to her, relationships were transactional. It was as if she was directing a twisted episode of the

TV show *Survivor*, where everyone around her served as captives that cannot leave—except she grants it.

I also knew that she had no right to call my husband to persuade him to get me to resign so she could hire another person. She also had no right to convince him to make me drop out of the doctoral program. The act was pure harassment. The next day, I talked to the lead counselor, a Black female that we all respected. She had worked in the district for years as a counselor and retired administrator. The principal rehired her to lead the counseling team. I told the lead counselor what had happened the previous day. I requested her to come with me to talk to the principal to know why she called my husband. I also wanted to make amends one way or the other to preserve our friendship and working relationship.

When we got to the principal's office, the lead counselor told her why we came and that she would like to mediate between us. The conversation became a heated argument because the principal refused to accept her wrong-doing, calling my husband. The principal repeated that she already told me that she gave me the job and wanted it back from me. She said I needed to resign or drop out of graduate school if I wanted to continue working for the district. I reminded her that I was qualified for the position and performed beyond her expectations before the issue started. I have worked and served her with all of my heart.

I then asked them, "What else do you want from me?"

The principal raised the issue of me going to the district to request a leave-of-absence without her consent. I asked her if that was why she called my husband, and she got quiet. I told her that she crossed the line. No district document or policy stated that a supervisor could call a family member on a case regarding this issue. At this point, the principal asked me these questions.

I still remember them vividly, "Do you want me to contact the HR Director to ask if they granted you the leave-of-absence?"

I responded, ".., we are both smart Black women. If there is a place in the district policies that states a supervisor can contact HR on behalf of their staff to make such an inquiry, I guess you can. However, if there is no such statement in the policy, please allow me to inquire myself."

The principal then asked a second question, "Would you resign if the district does not grant you the leave-of-absence?"

I responded, "I will cross that bridge when we get there."

At the end of the meeting, the principal was not happy about the responses I gave to her and the fact that she could not get me to resign. I couldn't avoid her the few days left in the school year. The admin meetings became unbearable and strained. With much fear, I attended the remaining few days as I waited for HR's response. The Superintendent and the Board granted me the one-year leave-of-absence to complete all my doctorate coursework. I was so grateful to have escaped an environment that seemed like one ruled by an authoritarian who wanted to control my dreams and aspirations. They wouldn't be mine anymore if the principal continued to control my mind.

I was able to take classes during the two summer sessions in 2016, both the fall and spring semesters in 2017, and the two summer sessions that year.

In July of 2017, The HR Executive Director called me to confirm if I would be comfortable returning to the same campus. I responded that I would be fine working with the Black female principal. Two weeks into the start of work for the administrators, the principal got a job in the district. The position was to lead the schools on the side of town, where most Black and Brown students reside. I thought this would be an opportunity to start again with a new principal, but I was wrong. My 'so-called friend' had given the latest White male principal the dossier she compiled based on her perspective. Soon after the White male principal assumed campus position, he revealed his views and philosophy regarding racial diversity. Quickly, I realized he saw no value in me as an immigrant. An accounting of my experiences with the White male principal and how he racially profiled me is in chapter four.

CHAPTER 3 DISCUSSION QUESTIONS

- What do you think about the actions of the Black female principal?

- If you were the assistant principal, how would you handle the call to your husband with your supervisor?

- What are the provisions in school law regarding principals calling their staffs' spouses to convince them about work-related issues?

- As a legal practitioner, Human Resources personnel, or Superintendent, what steps would you take if this report came to your attention?

HOW LEADERS PROJECT THEIR PERCEPTION OF EDUCATORS OF COLOR AS WORTHLESS

Most organizations and institutions put in the efforts to employ some people of color to show they embrace diversity. However, the leaders' perception regarding the value they attach to the people of color dictates their worth to others within the organization or institution. An organization that values diversity would embrace differences and celebrate individuals' uniqueness that makes up their teams. Most school district leaders are not different from other organizations that find it difficult to accept those they perceive differently. Rejecting diversity in its fullest form usually stunts the growth of an organization. Embracing others opens the door for the influx of innovative thinking and the team, organization, or institution's development.

Organizations and institutions that uphold the dominant culture's ideologies cage themselves into continuing business as usual and not see things from others' viewpoints. It can create a culture and climate that becomes toxic and unbearable for those treated differently and seen as outcasts. My experience with the White male principal made me question how he perceived me. What was I worth to him? Really?

As stated in chapter three, the Black female principal got a district office position to lead some schools about two weeks into the new school year. The district appointed a White male principal who was the principal of a middle school before this appointment.

The former Black female principal, who became a district administrator, reconnected with me outside of work through another mutual friend. We met for dinner. After dinner, I had to ride with her back home since she brought me to the restaurant. I was going through marriage separation before the divorce. On the way to my house, we talked to catch up, and the Black female district administrator apologized for the part she played that affected my marriage. She referred to the phone call and her words to my ex-husband that made my life hell with him. She also mentioned that she felt terrible that she mistreated me at work while I was going through my marital issues. I accepted her apology but was cautious, knowing she viewed relationships as a transaction. She sounded sincere, but an inner voice warned me not to get closer to her.

I wished I ran miles away from her in retrospection, especially with her new appointment as a district administrator. She inquired about the new White male principal and told me to be careful. She shared that she heard the White male principal discriminated against people of color. A White female teacher also confirmed that the White male principal discriminated against people of color when he was the middle school principal.

Although the Black female district administrator expressed that the White male principal discriminates, I also knew she most likely discussed me and shared stuff with the new principal. It is a known fact that the outgoing principal usually gives pointers and discusses issues and people with the incoming person. After this meeting, the Black district administrator and I frequently communicated on the phone. A BIG MISTAKE!

The White male principal met with all the AP's individually. In preparation for my meeting with him, I organized my department's data. I also had the initial goals I planned on sharing with the team to guide us as we collaborate on the final goals. The new principal's reaction and lack of enthusiasm indicated he was not interested in the instructional data I presented to him. He had a different plan and wanted information on my circle of friends.

One of the questions the White male principal asked me that surprised me was, "who are the people in your inner circle?"

I knew he was trying to profile me, place some worth on me by knowing my confidants.

I responded, "my children..." and chuckled to hide my discomfort.

He apparently couldn't sense my unease or just oblivious.

He probed further, "Who are your confidants at work? Who do you talk to about stuff at work?"

I told him that I maintained professionalism and talked to everyone I needed to take care of all our students and parents. After this meeting, I sensed the microaggressive behaviors the White male principal projected towards me. The White male principal ignored me and any contributions I made on several occasions during admin meetings. His microaggressions progressively became overt, racially discriminatory behaviors. An example was when I went to his office to request if I could apply to a district training institute for aspiring campus leaders shortly after school started in August of 2017.

My meeting with the White male principal this particular day was heart-wrenching. I told him my intention to apply and that I would appreciate it if I could list him as one of my references. He told me that he did not think the district would select me. I asked him if he felt I needed to change anything I was doing or improve for a better chance. The White male principal then asked me if I wanted him to tell me the truth. I responded, yes, please. He said that other AP's on the team have better chances than I did. He further stated that district administrators had concerns about making me a campus principal because of my accent.

The White male principal continued, "Yes, you are intelligent and capable of doing the job. However, no one will take the risk of putting you in such a position because of the community."

The district leaders fear the reactions of community members and would not risk upsetting them.

I left his office feeling down and confused. So, do I have to change my accent and my color? Which of these perceived issues can I fix and improve upon to move forward in my career?

As I drove home after work that day, I spoke to the Black district administrator, the former Black female principal, on the phone. I shared the awkward conversation I had with my new principal with her. I needed to talk to someone. I also wanted to ask her if I could list her as one of my references since she was my previous supervisor, and she agreed. A couple of weeks after these events, I heard back from the program's district coordinator that I got into the aspiring leaders' institute. In my excitement, I went to the White male principal's office to share the good news and to thank him for the reference he gave me. His response reflected anger and disapproval that I got into the program.

He said, "I did not give you a reference. I only gave ... (name of a White male assistant principal) a reference. (Name of the Black female district administrator) must have given you because I have already told you no one in the district will make you a principal."

Distraught and miserable, I quietly left his office. I called my former principal to let her know about the issue in my haze.

The White male principal's cold treatment and the ignoring continued during our meetings. I kept mute most of the time and just listened to everybody else because the White male principal kept acting like he couldn't understand what I said each time I spoke. Another major incident happened months later.

The administrator that coordinated the Advanced Placement (AP) Parent Information Night had a family emergency a few days before the event in January 2018. The principal sent a text to the admin team to know who could do the presentation. A Hispanic male assistant principal responded first to the group text message. The principal sent a confirmation text back to him. I also texted to express that I would co-present with the Hispanic male assistant principal. However, the principal did not respond to my request. I thought his silence meant I could co-present with the other AP, and I believed the other admin team members thought so. Because the next day, the Hispanic male assistant principal met with me to plan for the parent night. I suggested inviting students enrolled in Advanced Placement and DUAL Credit courses to share their experiences and how they managed academics with extracurricular activities. My thought process was that incoming parents and students would learn more directly from the students. They would be able to ask questions and get direct answers to lessen their concerns. The students did an excellent job, and the event was successful.

After the presentation, one of the parents walked up to me to thank me and then asked if I did anything wrong to offend the principal. I replied, no, and asked why? The parent said that the White male principal looked furious each time I talked, and his face turned all red. I told the parent that it was nothing; everything was fine. To confirm the parent's claims, I asked a female assistant principal if she saw what the parent described happened. She also said she noticed the same reactions whenever I talked. At first, I could not ask the principal about the incident to know if what the parent and the other assistant principal saw was true until another event took place. I met with the White male principal to inform him I was interested in applying for a principal position in one of the district's high schools. The principal discouraged me as usual. He said the district leaders would not consider me for the job. I thanked him but still applied for it.

A few days later, I received the Hire Vue, a virtual interview, and participated. To keep my principal in the loop of things, I informed him that I got an interview and thanked him again for the support and his reference. He retorted that he already told me he did not and would not give me a recommendation. The principal stated that the Black female district administrator probably helped me get to the interview stage. His words indicated he did not believe I could

46

perform well in interviews because my accent was of no value. However, to be sure of what I thought he was suggesting, I asked him to help me understand what he meant. He responded that he already told me that the district leaders would not put me in front of the community and parents because of my accent. Immediately, I remembered what the parent said they saw during the AP Parent Information Night.

At that point, I asked him if that was why he reacted to me each time I talked during the AP Parent Night? I told him a parent informed me because they thought I had done something wrong, and they could not understand why my principal looked mad each time I talked. The principal lost control and started yelling very angrily at me.

He then asked me, "Why were you there in the first place? I did not respond to your text message when you texted that you would help with the presentation because your face was not supposed to be seen by the parents."

He further stated, "Yes, maybe that was the anger the parent saw on my face. You were not supposed to be there." I was shocked!

I said, "But I am one of the Advanced Placement ambassadors' sponsors, and I had to be there to support our kids."

The principal responded, "Yes, you organized the students to talk. But do you have to be there, and if you are, do you need to talk?"

Then, I asked him if he was serious about the issue with my accent. The principal said yes. I told him that he gave me feedback that my accent was a problem, but I'm sorry, I cannot change it, but I can work on it. The principal got angry again.

In a fury, he replied, "When I started as the principal here (mentioned three top district personnel and the former Black female principal) called me and went down the list of admin team members that they can never make a campus leader. Your name was one mentioned, and they all said you are intelligent, but they cannot put you in the position because of your accent."

Then he asked me after he calmed down from being angry, "So are you going to file a grievance against me?"

He tried to justify his actions and words and stated that he gave me honest feedback, and he said I did not seem to like it. I was so hurt and troubled. I believe he saw the tears and disappointment on my face.

Then he asked, "Are you going to file a grievance against me?"

I responded, "I do not operate in this way; if I wanted to file a grievance, I would have done so. All I wanted was for us to make amends and work together. I may have an accent, but I get my work done."

I cried so hard that day.

I know those reading would be wondering why I did not file the grievance understanding the principal's actions were a clear Title VI violation. Well, I was scared and felt defeated. I had no political power to go against him and those mentioned in the district. I felt powerless, deflated, and subdued.

After this incident, I kept mute because I was scared of retaliation and could not report it. The principal's behavior made me feel I was his target, and he wanted me off his campus to bring people who looked like him to be part of his team. My experience with this White male principal was very hurtful. His act of prejudice was overt. He saw no value in me and did not hide his feelings towards me. I realized that my only option was to transfer. I discussed my thoughts with the Black female district administrator. She offered to talk to a White female middle school principal with an open position in one of the schools she supervised. I requested a district transfer to the middle school. Another mistake! In hindsight, I realized the Black female district administrator, my so-called friend, only helped with the transfer because she wanted to monitor my progress and perhaps find a new way for me to pull my hair out!

The middle school principal wanted a Black assistant principal to show the community her diversity efforts after a disciplinary scandal that involved a White assistant principal and a Black student. The White assistant principal resigned because the parent filed grievances against the campus administration. I also later found out that the White female principal worked as an assistant principal with the White male high school principal I ran from to avoid continued harassment. The White female middle school principal started with subtle micro-aggressions shortly after I joined the campus. She even recruited a handful of White teachers to harass me whenever I advocated for students of color. I will elaborate on the different ways the White female principal exhibited unethical behaviors and got away with them in chapter five.

CHAPTER 4 DISCUSSION QUESTIONS

- What would you have done if you were the Black female assistant principal working with the White male principal?

- Discuss how the scenario in this chapter violates Title VI of the Civil Rights Act. What rights do educators and students of color have, and how are they protected under Title VI?

- As a district legal adviser, how would you handle this situation to address the possible violations of Title VI of the Civil Rights Act?

- As the district human resource personnel and superintendent, how would you handle this situation?

HOW SCHOOL DISTRICTS SUPPORT THE UNETHICAL BEHAVIORS OF CAMPUS LEADERS

Most organizations and institutions continue to support the unethical behaviors of those that are in leadership positions. They refuse to hold them accountable, or they trivialize the issue, especially when it involves racial equity to protect policies grounded in whiteness. Organizations and institutions sweep most problems involving racial injustice under the carpet instead of dealing with them. Ignoring or covering the issues gives the leaders the impression that it is okay for them to act unjustly. Some school district leaders also support campus leaders' unethical behaviors and sweep the complaints under the carpet to avoid negative media coverage. The policies they create to address unjust actions on school campuses are unfair, leaving the victims no other choice but to be quiet or blacklist them.

Several school district policies create a chilling effect on staff and parents. An example is allowing the campus principal to be the hearing officer of a grievance submitted to the district office by an employee on that same campus or one by a parent. The district refers to the first grievance as a level one, and campus principals handle such issues. How can the person the victim is reporting be the judge of the case? It makes no sense and creates a "chilling effect" and barriers that stop individuals from pursuing justice. The district will uphold the campus principal's ruling if the employee insists on going through the grievance process. The employee has no choice but to either accept it or opt to file a level two grievance.

At this point, human resources (HR) moves to appoint a representative to hear the case. The campus leaders know that HR will consistently support them. Therefore, they have no sense of accountability and act privileged to commit various acts of hostility on their campuses at the expense of other educators' careers. School leaders maltreat and emotionally stifle educators of color in the same or similar ways organizations and other institutions mistreat people of color. Leaders use different strategies to keep victims quiet or punished when they stand against maltreatment. Some of the various methods used to uphold whiteness are tokenism, exclusion from decision-making, micro-aggression, harassment, intimidation, and negative narratives. The following sections highlight my experiences with the White female middle school principal. She used different ways to stifle me emotionally.

Tokenism

As explained in chapter four, the district and middle school campus leaders needed a Black face as a façade to convince and show the community the school administration's diversity efforts. However, the reality was that I was just a face to make the parents of students of color feel better and comfortable when they visited the campus. The White female principal deprived me of the privilege to participate in decision-making. I had several conversations with parents of color regarding how the teachers and administration treated their kids like criminals. Most school leaders use educators of color viewed as tokens to clean up the racially charged messes they create due to their discriminatory acts. This White female principal was more concerned about the teachers' comfort than students' experiences/safety and encouraged the students of color's continued criminalization. The principal talked about equity, 'capturing kids' hearts,' and restorative discipline. However, she could not hold teachers accountable and gave them everything they wanted to be 'liked' by them. She did not consider what was best for the students. I will share two incidents of the several that happened during the three years I worked there. I feel pained and troubled each time I remember these occurrences.

The first incident was the arrest of a sixth-grader, a Black male student put in handcuffs by the City Police Officer. The student got into a physical altercation with a White male student. It started in a teacher's classroom and spilled into the hallway during passing period. The White student pushed the Black student, who then went after him and punched him. The assistant principal and the principal, both White women, encouraged the White parent to file charges against the Black student with no history of violence. After the police took the boy away in handcuffs, I went into my office and cried so hard. I felt helpless and could not stop them from taking him. I questioned the assistant principal and the principal's roles in the whole situation. Could they have mediated between both parents without encouraging the White parent to file the assault charges against the Black student? I still question how they both handled it. I know that administrators that care about students of color would have mediated between parents and students to discourage police involvement. Administrators that care would think about the student's future and how arrest records and such a traumatic encounter with the law affect the students of color from such an early age to adulthood.

The second incident that shocked me and had me speechless was when my principal came into my office with a White female inclusion education teacher. They talked about a female Hispanic student who received additional instructional services. They both recommended that I send the student to the Alternative Education Program/Campus (AEP). They stated that the student walked around the campus like she owned it and skipped classes. They both also said they've counted the number of office discipline referrals teachers wrote. The student had enough to warrant her removal to the alternative school, but discretionally. Hearing these statements from the White female principal and the inclusion education teacher stunned me to no end. Their demand confirmed why campus and district data continued to show the disparity in the representation of students of color amongst those disciplined or removed on a discretionary basis to the AEP.

The teacher was the student's liaison and was supposed to know how to meet the student's educational needs and have a relationship with her to understand why she skipped classes. I informed them that I was working with the student, parent, and teachers. The student shared that she felt the teachers did not like her and always picked on her. But they both insisted that they did not want the student on the campus. At this point, I asked the teacher to write the referral and call the parent. I also requested the principal write a note that she recommended the student's removal from the middle school campus to the discipline alternative education campus. I told them that I would count the number of days the student was out of placement due to in and out-of-school suspensions previously assigned that school year to comply with the requirements. I became frustrated because I gave the in and out-of-school suspensions (ISS & OSS) due to the teachers' complaints to the principal that I was not supporting their punitive disciplinary ways of intervention. Both the principal and the teacher did not like my response. They expected me to initiate and take responsibility to send the student discretionally to the alternative campus.

I believe in Capturing Kids' Hearts and struggled with why adults could be so vindictive. Their request indicated their reluctance to work with students. They failed to reflect on how they engaged with the students in the classrooms to make them feel accepted and comfortable in class. The teacher did not write the referral. She avoided the call to the student's parents, knowing they would push back on the referral. Also, the principal avoided writing the comment. She knew it would be a difficult case to defend. However, she wanted to use me as a Black assistant principal to send students of color to an alternative school to protect herself from critics. As a White woman, operating from a whiteness lens, she needed a token to take the fall and wanted my name on it. At the same time, she intentionally excluded me from other decision-makings and meetings.

Exclusion

Individuals appointed to tokenized positions lack permission to make decisions. Organization and institution leaders only involve or permit them to contribute to specific issues, especially contentious ones, to shift the burden on the tokenized person. The leaders avoid taking responsibility for any adverse outcomes from the decisions made and would rather have a token fall from the consequences. The White female principal also intentionally excluded me from both formal and informal meetings. She made plans with the other two White female assistant principals on professional developments. When I requested to participate, they responded that they have already planned what they will present to staff. The principal interviewed several candidates for three teaching positions in the department I supervised three consecutive times without involving me. The first time it happened, the White female principal told me she forgot she did not invite me, even though I would be supervising the teacher. However, she invited a couple of teachers and another assistant principal that supervised another department. The second time it happened, I requested a meeting with the principal. I invited a substitute assistant principal that joined the team after one of the female assistant principals left for a teaching position. Coincidentally, the substitute assistant principal was the same retired principal and counselor that I asked to mediate between my former Black female principal and me. The White female principal claimed it was an oversight, even though it happened twice. The same incident occurred not too long after the meeting. Another new teacher's interview came up, and the person came on board my department without my involvement in the interview process. To top it off, the principal put an interview team together to interview for the third assistant principal position. She left me out of the plans to interview candidates. I did not know the date and time. I learned about the meeting on the morning of the scheduled interviews when a teacher asked if I would be present. This White female principal's act to intentionally exclude me from these interviews indicated her desire to isolate me. She created and continued to sustain a situation of "them against me" that existed before the White female assistant principal left. They recruited the Hispanic male assistant principal that joined their "them against me" team. The principal failed to consider that I would be on the same team as the new assistant principal. These actions reflected leaders' behaviors that encourage harassment and victimization in their organizations and institutions through exclusions.

Microaggressions and Harassment

Individuals in tokenized positions experience micro-aggressions and subtle harassment when they pushback to participate in decision-making. Leaders of organizations and institutions who intentionally exclude tokenized individuals project microaggressive behaviors. Other workers take a cue from the leaders' actions. The leaders' silence, smiles, facial expressions, or words reaffirm other workers' microaggressive conduct. The White female principal exhibited negative leadership characteristics that encouraged a few of the teachers' negative behaviors. Her 'they against me' administrative team recruited a handful of willing White folks on campus to harass me subtly or overtly continually. The Hispanic male assistant principal was very eager to act as instructed by the White female principal and the White female assistant principal. They were his mentors, being his first year as an assistant principal. He wanted to belong and get their approval. He worked against students of color and other educators of color. He stalked me around the campus to know whom I was talking to, which classroom I went into, or who was in my office, student, or parent. His fixation compelled him to monitor me in a way 'to get me.' It was also to divert attention from his lack of experience and to cover up his inadequacies. They recruited two White female teachers and encouraged their insubordination acts and overt harassment because they could not find any fault in my performance.

One of those recruited was a special education behavior intervention teacher. The teacher openly challenged every decision I made and would yell at me. One such occurrence was when I allowed a parent and her three children into the commons area after school to wait for the gym to open for the games. She yelled at me in front of the parent to let me know I had no right to let them in and should have left them in the rain or asked them to go through the back door that led to the gym area. The parent felt sorry for me because I was speechless. The parent called the school the next day and requested to talk to the principal to plead on behalf of the Black staff member (me). The parent thought the White female teacher who yelled at me was the principal and was scared I would lose my job for letting them into the building. The parent narrated the event to the principal, so I would not get punished for helping her and her children. The principal disregarded the parent's call and did not reprimand the teacher for insubordination. The teacher's micro and macroaggressions continued, and I actively and intentionally avoided her.

The second teacher recruited by the 'them against me' team was a White female coach. She was one of the teachers that assisted with the cafeteria supervision during lunch duty. However, she always came late. When I addressed the issue with her and other coaches, she claimed the principal approved her lateness to the cafeteria. She stated that she was late because she monitored the girls' locker room before they came for lunch. I brought the issue to the principal's attention. I told her what the coach said. I also expressed my wonderings that the students the coach claimed she was monitoring were the same in the cafeteria at the same time. Also, the other two female coaches came for duties before her. The principal said she would talk to the coach to be on time for cafeteria duty.

The same White female coach wrote office discipline referrals on students with inaccurate narratives. I discovered several times during investigations as I talked to students and other coaches that witnessed the incidents. The other coaches also told me that she embellished and lied when she had conversations with others to cover her faults. Several parents, not just parents of students of color but also White parents, brought numerous complaints about her to me since I was the 8th-grade assistant principal. I tried as much as I could to manage her inaccurate narratives and not punish students unfairly. The decisions or consequences I assigned students after investigations continued to prove her false accounts of events and made her unhappy with me.

A parent reported the coach to me regarding her false allegations against a White female student. The parent requested a teacher-parent conference. The principal appointed the White female assistant principal to join the parent-teacher meeting without my prior knowledge. They claimed the coach didn't want to meet with the White female parent and me without the other White female assistant principal. After the meeting, the principal and the two assistant principals on the 'them against me' team encouraged the coach to write a grievance against me for 'harassment and sarcasm.' The coach was mad because questioning her actions to understand what actually happened and why she falsely accused the student exposed her lies. The principal's office staff members witnessed the principal's, assistant principals', and the coach's plans to write a grievance against me. They informed me that the principal invited the coach to her office to help with writing and to file the grievance. Since it was a level I grievance, the principal knew she would be the hearing officer. She had the power to control the narratives and make the decision to support the story. Like other leaders of organizations and institutions, the White female principal's desperation to stifle me emotionally and maintain the dominant culture's ideologies compelled her vindictive actions.

Negative Narratives and Falsification of Records

Many school leaders victimize educators of color who advocate for students of color to stop them from advocating to maintain their dominant culture's ideologies. Their desperations make them commit errors and disregard laws and rules because their Whiteness gives them a sense of entitlement that they are untouchable. Like most organizations and institutions, these leaders get away with these abuses of power because Human Resources and other organization leaders cover up the negative behaviors and blame the victims. They re-enforce the terrible actions to maintain the ideologies of the dominant culture.

The White female principal's desperation to write negative narratives about me in the grievance document came to my knowledge when I caught them red-handed. They added negative statements to the Google document they shared with me as part of the grievance hearing they claimed the coach wrote. As God would have it, I witnessed the principal adding comments to the statements while reviewing the content on Sunday, the day after they shared it with me via email. When I saw that the principal was typing the negative comments, I immediately sent them the text message below to inquire and confirm in writing:

"..., were you the one editing the athletic director's request, adding "and a non-threatening tone" after the word sarcasm? I saw your log-in details, and you logged out after I placed my cursor on yours to let you know I saw you."

The White female principal's response after a long pause of cursor blinking was:

"Yes. I realized I was on the document I shared with you, and yes I doctored and deleted what was added. I told her to make it more explicit so that you know exactly what she wants from the grievance. The AD did not do it, so I helped her out. I have already printed and attached the originals to the grievance, which will be in the big meeting. Those are the original ones I shared with you the other day. What she wrote was kind of inane and unprecise, and I want you to know exactly what she is asking for, so there is no confusion. Nothing will change from what I shared with you. They are already printed in my office. I have a separate folder with a copy for you already. This is not my first rodeo with a grievance, and I'm proceeding based on experience... Let's meet up when you get to school in the afternoon tomorrow."

So, think about it, if the perpetrator is also the judge of the case, what do you think the verdict would be? Apart from the principal's vindictive attempts, their desperate actions to write negative narratives against me exposed their ineffectiveness as a leader. However, their privilege as a White woman and a campus principal encouraged them to continue with the false accusations. I know some readers must be wondering what I did upon discovering they made changes to the submitted document. I contacted her supervisor, the Black female district administrator I discussed in chapter two, the former Black female high school principal. They said the White female principal would be the hearing officer because it is a Level I grievance. I shared the text message that confirmed the White female principal was already biased and their plot to set me up—I told the Black female district administrator that the White principal's action was a breach and misuse of their office and power.

The Black female district administrator responded:

"It is a fissure, but it's not one we can't step over."

The 'we' they referred to was the district leadership. I also asked if I decided to write a grievance to counter what the opposition submitted if another district personnel would be the hearing officer? The Black female district administrator responded that the White female principal will still be the hearing officer. Getting these responses confirmed that some district leaders support the unethical behaviors of campus leaders.

The Black female district administrator empowered the White female principal even when they falsified information to defame my character. They knew the district would support their actions and their unethical behaviors, which are punishable under Texas Educators and Administrative Codes. Falsification of records and defamation of character could result in termination of appointment.

The White female principal's actions offering me a tokenized position as the only Black female administrator on their campus, at the same time excluding me from decision making, including their encouragement and participation in micro-aggression, harassment, intimidation, and negative narratives against me upheld the ideologies of the dominant culture. The principal saw the need to keep me quiet or punish me for advocating for students and parents of color to maintain the Whiteness.

Most leaders of organizations and institutions frustrate people of color in different ways to subdue them; likewise, school leaders frustrate educators of color that advocate for students. The district leaders, including Human Resources, continue to encourage the campus leaders' unethical behaviors and cover up the scandals. The leaders put the burden of proof on the victim and do not hold the perpetrators accountable for their actions. They give the benefits of the doubt to the perpetrator and not the victim to maintain white supremacy culture and power.

CHAPTER 5 DISCUSSION QUESTIONS

- If you were the Black female assistant principal, what could you have done differently to mitigate the situation?

- What would you do if you were the Black female district administrator and an assistant principal reached out to you about the situation above to ensure fairness?

- As a district legal adviser, how would you handle this situation?

- As the district human resource personnel, how would you handle this situation?

- Which policies in your institution can you examine to ensure these situations cannot occur and to ensure the safety of employees of color?

HOW THE INTERSECTION OF POWER, POLITICS, LEADERSHIP, AND RACE UPHOLD DOMINANT CULTURE'S IDEOLOGIES

Reflecting on my public school system experiences, I continue to analyze how individuals' power, politics, and leadership skills intersect. In these experiences, working with different leaders, Black, Hispanic, and White; male and female, as presented in the last five chapters, a glaring light is shed on the intersection of power, politics, leadership, and race.

Most organizations and institutions maintain power through racial inequities within the organizational structures. A few people of color usually occupy tokenized administrative or managerial positions, generally not more than glorified placeholders to strengthen the dominant culture's governance. In this dynamics, tokenized individuals always watch over their shoulders to continually ensure they serve the interest of those who appointed them and that they don't buck the status quo. For the most part, they often never fully entirely come unto their authority as they feel they are continuously being micromanaged and evaluated. Whether the feelings experienced by the tokenized individuals are real or not, it speaks to the lack of confidence existing between races. The situation usually results in an environment where the person of color appointed as tokens finds it difficult to exercise the authority conferred by their position altogether. They are incapacitated and unable to fully apply the benefits of their diverse experiences to offer maximum benefits to the organization. They often have two options most of the time. They either follow the mainstream ideology of whiteness and work against other people of color to subdue them or advocate for them, resulting in losing their jobs.

Individuals that occupy positions of power, regardless of their race, also understand the political landscape of the organization they lead. They know the players and those they can recruit to propagate and strengthen their agenda. Individuals with excellent leadership skills with visions and goals aligned with the organization and who believe in racial equity can move the organization with a progressive mindset without boundaries. However, individuals who occupy positions of power, with their selfish agendas, can impact the organization to support and uphold the dominant culture ideology marginalizing people of color. This group of leaders lacks effective leadership qualities because they are operating from a selfish point of view.

Examples of essential leadership skills are integrity, ability to delegate effectively, clear communication, appreciation, respect for all, self-awareness, self-control, and empathy. Other qualities are the courage to lead in truth, influence others to do what is equitable, just, and right, and the ability to be life-long learners. From my observations and experiences working with the three leaders I discussed in the previous chapters, they lack these qualities.

The Black female principal that eventually became a district administrator was selfishly courageous and quite the enigma to figure out. However, her actions projected a very ambitious individual who lacks self-awareness, empathy and demands respect using fear to control subordinates. Her courage, political power, and relationships with other district administrators, including the Human Resources, further encouraged her to victimize, knowing there would be no consequences. As a woman of color, she upheld the dominant culture's ideology using the fear and victimization tactics to enslave and stifle her subordinates' emotions and performances.

The White male principal, on the other hand, did not hide his privileges and the space he occupied as a representative of the dominant culture. From my experiences working with him, he focused more on walking around campus to make friends – building social relationships but was not focused on academic leadership. I'm not against making friends; it is excellent. However, the work of a school administrator involves instructional leadership coupled with relationship building.

He was not an instructional leader. He lacked self-awareness, got angry, yelled, demanded what he wanted, and projected entitlement. He lacked proper communication when engulfed with anger. He also lacked empathy, did not care how their words affected others, especially one from a marginalized race. His behavior was paradoxical.

On the one hand, the White male principal wanted to form friendships with certain people in their "circle of friends," people that looked like him. On the other hand, he wanted people of color, like me, one with a Nigerian accent, excluded from campus leadership. He wanted me to be a token and do the heavy lifting for others but not be part of the faces that represented the school in meetings with the parents and community. He lacked respect and the ability to learn from others.

Lastly, the White female principal was able to hide her inability to lead as a courageous leader. She hid behind followers that volunteered to implement her biddings. She used her position and the associated political power to recruit willing educators to victimize those she did not like. Her action, falsifying information to defame my character, showed her desperation to victimize at any length. She lacked integrity. She projected that she knew her supervisor, the Black district administrator, and the human resources executive director would support her unethical behavior. When I inquired about the changes I caught her making to the grievance document, her response to my text message revealed her ineffectiveness as a leader and her lack of integrity.

From these experiences, I firmly believe school districts and other organizations need to make the process of diversity more robust. They should understand that diversity implementation can result in a paradox, contradicting the goals, when the process does not involve equity and inclusion. School districts also need to consider reviewing policies that do not support the implementation of diversity.

The section below describes the paradoxes of policy review, hiring for diversity, and creating an equity office. Most organizations and institutions usually mention these three elements as areas of focus to achieve diversity. However, the processes they implement negate their efforts due to the systemic racism and individuals who continue to uphold the dominant culture's ideology. Most of the policies surrounding these areas of focus result in systemic racism because they emanated only from the lens of whiteness.

The Paradox of Policy Review

Most school districts and organizations take pride in their attempts to review different policies to address equity issues, but usually, they do not consider those invited to review the policies. Even when people of color are part of the review committee, power dynamics subtly control decision-making. Those involved influence the agreement they would reach on what needs changing, how they will implement what they suggested, and how people will be accountable to the truth.

Whenever district leaders talk about policy review regarding diversity, equity, and inclusion, I ask myself the following questions: Who nominated the review committee members? What plans are they trying to push forward? Who are they advocating for, people of color or their selfish interests?

The committee may not achieve the expected outcomes if the review process is to satisfy the leaders' agenda. They may also fail if they intend to check the box to show the world, they made some attempts to change their policies. The policy review paradox reverts the attempts to what it used to be to uphold the dominant culture's ideology.

An essential policy that school districts, including the school board members, need to review and change is the grievance policy. There is a need for district personnel to be the hearing officer when staff or parents writes a grievance about the campus principal. The district personnel should be free of loyalty towards the campus principal to be fair in their decision-making. It makes no sense to have the principal sit and decide a case that alleged their wrongdoing. There should be an accountability process that holds campus leaders accountable for their actions, rather than placing the burden of proof on their victims.

The Paradox of Hiring to Diversify

The recent incidents and the country's progressive movements have compelled most organizations and institutions to change their hiring policies to diversify. Most organizations are also focusing on their managerial and executive positions. Most school districts use HireVue, a video interview software and platform to screen candidates after the resume screening—acting as the first level of the hiring process. The main question to ask regarding the hiring process is who nominates those that screen the applicant resumes? What criteria are they using to select candidates? If they are diversifying, what names are they intentionally or unintentionally avoiding? Like mine, Kehinde Olowoyeye might be repulsive to the hiring committee with a phobia for names that indicate African descent. They would most likely ignore these names and the credentials on the resume. Suppose the individual gets nominated for some reason. In that case, the second huddle is the HireVue that is very subjective, just like the face-to-face interview.

As a candidate and a hiring committee member, I have experienced both sides using the HireVue interview platform. For this book, I want to focus on my experience as a hiring committee member. The White female principal led the hiring team. She screened the resumes and nominated the search committee. From my perspective, the majority of those she chose agreed with her biddings. She picked me reluctantly to show human resources that she included me. After reviewing the candidates' resumes, their HireVue recorded responses, and their responses during the interviews, it was very apparent that a female Hispanic assistant principal had more experience and would be suitable for the position. The White female principal and assistant principal raised concerns about the female Hispanic candidate's accent and how the staff may not welcome her accent and tone. Once the hiring committee sensed that the principal and the White female assistant principal desired a male Hispanic candidate with less experience, they changed their opinions to align with what the principal wanted. The interview committee members - the teachers and the counselor, also claimed they were uncomfortable with the male and female African American candidates' tones. They said the teachers on campus would not like their 'tones.' These types of arguments only pointed to the expression of their fragility around people of color.

If this happened on a small scale and an individual in a position of power can influence the hiring process, then the same can happen on the district level. Even though districts and different organizations use the HireVue interview platform, the selection process is still subjective and skewed.

A common argument that decision-makers come up with when they end up hiring a white person for a position that they planned to fill with a person of color is that they could not find a person of color capable of doing the job. In short, they are saying they cannot "substitute efficiency with diversity," defeating the purpose of diversifying their workforce. They fail to understand that people of color may come for the interview with less experience due to the different barriers they encounter each day. Examples of the possible barriers to consider are geographical locations and the systemic structures and policies that restrict or disfranchise people of color from accessing opportunities the same way their white counterparts would easily do. Another barrier to consider is the candidate's network and their connections to those in power positions.

School district leaders should ask questions regarding who makes up hiring committees and how power dynamics could influence the hiring process.

The Paradox of the Equity Office

Creating an equity office does not necessarily equate to an organization or institution implement equitable policies. When a school district decides to create the equity office, what are their plans for the office? How much are they willing to allocate to support the office? Whom would they hire to lead the office? What power comes with the office? What types of involvement and decision-making capability would the office have regarding racial issues, especially when such issues relate to human resources and instruction?

I asked all the questions above because establishing an equity office within an organization and institution creates avenues to improve diversity. These measures can support the indigenous, people of color, LGBTQIA individuals, people with disabilities— including gifted & talented students in all schools. However, the office can only function properly when the right people occupy the office and are empowered by providing the resources needed. Suppose the district leaders perceive the Chief Equity Officer position as a token. In that case, they may not equip the office with enough funds and power. Limited power would not enable the equity office to advocate for staff and students, which contradicts the established equity office's purpose. The person appointed to the position could eventually be a product of the district's or organization's equity detour to create an illusion of their equity efforts.

Recommendations

As mentioned in chapter one, leaders of organizations and institutions have the best intentions to improve their workforce diversity. However, most of the actions implemented produce outcomes that contradict the goal to diversify. Based on my personal and professional experiences, I'm suggesting the following recommendations.

1. Leaders who are considering improving their workforce diversity need to be **intentional and purposeful**. They should understand there would be backlashes and pushbacks. Politically, they may lose their popularity, but they need to consider what is essential – their political positions, recognitions, or the students' lives. There is a need for them to self-reflect on their practices and their impacts on their workforce diversity.

2. Another great effort leaders check off as accomplished on their lists of actions they implement to diversify their workforce is providing ongoing professional developments to address racial equity or other forms of inequities. However, they do not put a plan in place to hold those they have trained accountable. **The accountability process should involve individuals' opportunities to self-reflect and assess how they implemented what they learned from the training and if it resulted in the desired changes on their campuses and departments**. There should also be a common language and understanding of what success would look like considering workforce diversity and its impact on student achievement.

3. Leaders should review hiring and retention policies with the intent to improve workforce diversity. **The retention process**

should include how the administration would protect people or teachers of color that report legitimate mistreatment incidents borne out of racial biases. Most of the time, the opposite is what happens. In their efforts to suppress the issue, leaders usually ignore or put the burden of proof on the person reporting the mistreatment. The supervisors, the perpetrator—all know that the organization's leaders would find ways to avoid the issue getting to the press to avoid bad publicity. Other educators of color have shared their experiences with me where the school districts supported campus principals, and the action left them helpless. One of them shared that they insisted that the district investigate the racial discrimination. When the school district's human resources started the investigation, they realized the issue was more significant than they thought. They hired a Black female lawyer that suddenly left in the middle of the investigation, and they did provide the educator the lawyer's findings. The school district hired another independent Black male lawyer. He also left mysteriously without providing the educator his conclusions. The educator shared that these investigations went on for over a year. The human resources and each of these lawyers met with the educator over twelve times, and they requested the educator to write a summary of the answers they gave to all the questions asked. The Black educator expressed the emotional trauma they experienced. The educator could not afford a lawyer, and at the same time, wanted the mistreatment to stop. The school district did not come up with any concrete results. There was no closure. They moved the educator to another campus to silence them and make the whole thing go away. School district leaders have and continue to silence many educators of color that feel helpless while the school district leaders continue to embolden the perpetrators through their actions to make the complaint go away by frustrating the victims.

4. Finally, **school districts and organizations must ensure their Equity Office gets involved in resolving staff's**

mistreatment at the initial phase of the complaint. Most of the time, the human resources personnel that handle racial issues do not have enough racial competence to develop and maintain healthy cross-racial relationships required to resolve the issue. Therefore, they cannot analyze the racial dynamics and confront the acts of racism inherent in the case they are investigating. Most times, the human resources' loyalty to the perpetrator and the district's or organization's leaders cloud their judgment. Allowing the Equity Office to get involved at the initial stage could help resolve the issue to make the complainant feel heard, and the campus leader or supervisor understand where they went wrong and how they can repair the harm they caused to save the relationship. It is important to note that school districts can achieve this kind of resolve if the Equity Office(r) is not part of their equity detour, but they are supported and given the right resources to carry out their functions within the school district or organization.

In conclusion, leaders of organizations understand the intersection of power, politics, and race. Their knowledge of the organization's political landscape and the power that comes with their position makes it possible for them to uphold policies ingrained in racism. As shown in the example discussed in chapter three, the leader's race did not necessarily make her consider how her actions upheld the dominant culture's ideology. Her ambitions drove her actions; she willingly supported and sustained the dominant ideology and marginalized other people of color. It is also essential that organizations and educational institutions review and reform policies that perpetuate racism.

I hope this book informs universities and colleges that prepare future educators in their undergraduate and graduate programs on the impact of policies and systemic racial inequities on teachers and administrators of color. I also hope the scenarios narrated in each chapter would prompt discussions amongst students and professors who teach different teacher, principal, and superintendent preparation programs. Likewise, I hope this book would inform district and campus administrators, Human Resources, counselors, and the district legal department to implement equitable policies and provide diversity training to staff members.

ABOUT THE AUTHOR

Kehinde Olowoyeye has been serving as a public school educator for over sixteen years. She was a science teacher for seven years before becoming an assistant principal in 2012. She has had the privilege to work in this administrative role in the middle and comprehensive high schools, including the alternative high school. She has served on various campus and school district committees, such as a school district's Equity Task Force. Her collaborative work with others and contributions to the equity task force resulted in the district's hiring of the first Equity Officer. She teaches ESL classes as an adjunct instructor at Austin Community College in the Adult Education Department.

Kehinde blends her passions for equity and instructional leadership through her research to inform her practices and others.

She conducted a study for her campus and district in 2012 on the low representation of students of color in Advanced Placement Courses. The study's findings changed the enrollment practices. Her first published work was her dissertation in 2018 – "High School Leaders' Sensemaking, Actions, and Practices in Reducing the Overrepresentation of Students of Color in Disciplinary Alternative Education Program."

Kehinde holds a Doctor of Philosophy in Educational Leadership and Policy and a Master of Educational Administration from The University of Texas at Austin. She has a Master of Education with a concentration in Biology from Lincoln University, PA. She had her first postgraduate (MS) and undergraduate (BA) degrees in Botany from the University of Lagos and the University of Ilorin, Nigeria, where she grew up. She served as an assistant lecturer at the University of Lagos.

Kehinde desires to continue developing and supporting teachers to serve all students equitably. She also provides training on workforce diversity. You can reach her at:

Kehinde.olowo12@gmail.com
Kehinde.olowoyeye@cequityec.com
LinkedIn linkedin.com/in/kehinde-olowoyeye-ph-d-67301221
Twitter @kolowoy

www.ingramcontent.com/pod-product-compliance
Lightning Source LLC
Chambersburg PA
CBHW060318100426
42812CB00003B/819